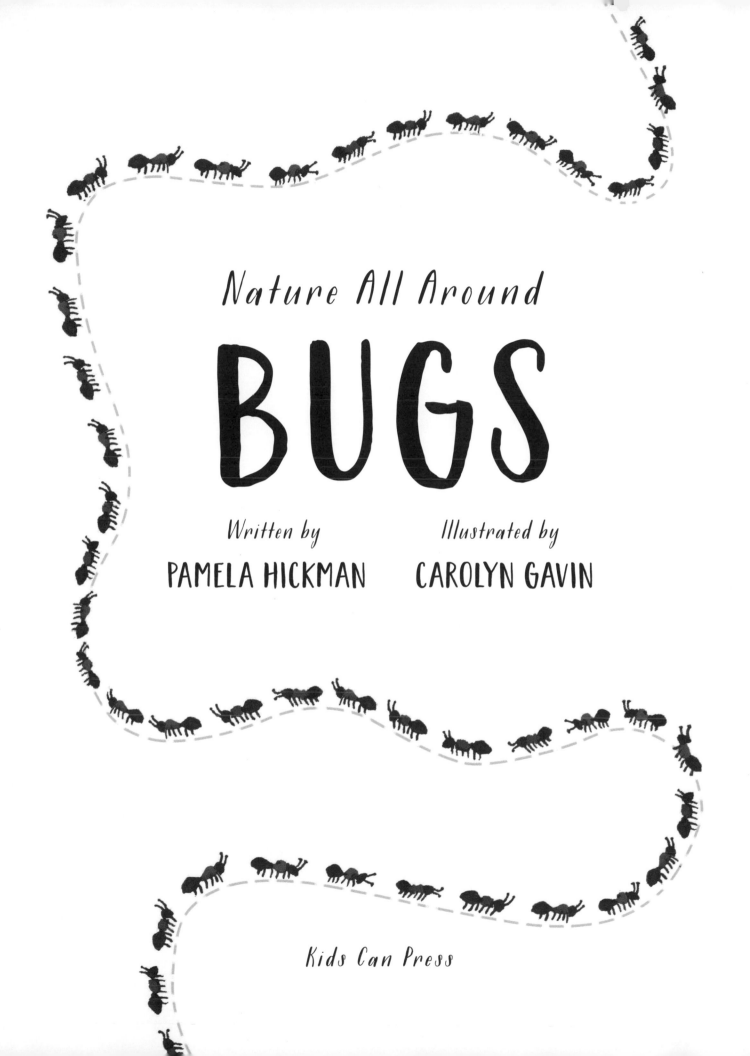

Nature All Around

BUGS

Written by
PAMELA HICKMAN

Illustrated by
CAROLYN GAVIN

Kids Can Press

For Rosie, with love from Nana — P.H.

For my family, who put up with me during intense work days, and for Mother Nature, for designing such beautiful bugs to paint — C.G.

Acknowledgments

Big thanks to Karen Powers, the designer, who was full of direction and guidance throughout the project — *C.G.*

Published in Canada and the U.S. by Kids Can Press Ltd.
25 Dockside Drive, Toronto, ON M5A 0B5

Kids Can Press is a Corus Entertainment Inc. company

The artwork in this book was rendered in watercolor and gouache. The text is set in Kepler.

Edited by Katie Scott and Kathleen Keenan
Designed by Karen Powers

Printed and bound in Shenzhen, China, in 4/2023 by C & C Offset

MIX
Paper | Supporting responsible forestry
FSC® C008047
www.fsc.org

CM 19 09876543

Library and Archives Canada Cataloguing in Publication

Hickman, Pamela, author
    Bugs / written by Pamela Hickman ; illustrated by Carolyn Gavin.

(Nature all around ; 2)
Includes index.
Based on content previously published in The kids Canadian bug book
    (Toronto: Kids Can Press, 1996), and Starting with nature bug book
    (Toronto: Kids Can Press, 1999).
ISBN 978-1-77138-820-7 (hardcover)

    1. Insects — Juvenile literature. I. Gavin, Carolyn, illustrator II. Title.

QL467.2.H495 2019   j595.7   C2018-905842-0

Kids Can Press gratefully acknowledges that the land on which our office is located is the traditional territory of many nations, including the Mississaugas of the Credit, the Anishnabeg, the Chippewa, the Haudenosaunee and the Wendat peoples, and is now home to many diverse First Nations, Inuit and Métis peoples.

We thank the Government of Ontario, through Ontario Creates; the Ontario Arts Council; the Canada Council for the Arts; and the Government of Canada for supporting our publishing activity.

Contents

Bugs Are All Around

Have you seen a bug today? Maybe you noticed ants on a sidewalk, a ladybug on a plant or a butterfly gliding through the air. Wherever you live, you are sure to find bugs nearby.

There are twice as many insects in the world as all other kinds of animals combined. Many animals, such as fish, birds, frogs, turtles and bats, depend on insects for food. And plants need insects to carry pollen from one flower to another (called pollination) to produce seeds that will grow into new plants. Without insect pollinators, we couldn't grow many of the fruits and vegetables we eat. Take a look at the bugs throughout these pages to discover more about these fascinating creatures.

 Look out for the "Strange Bugs" sections to discover some truly bizarre insects!

What's the difference between an insect and a true bug? Turn the page to find out!

Check out some insect impostors, like millipedes and worms, on pages 8–9. Can you find the impostor on this page?

Find out how to make an insect feeder on page 29.

Learn how to identify bugs with the questionnaire on pages 24–25.

Bugs Up Close

Bugs come in an amazing variety of shapes, sizes and colors. They may look different from one another, but they all have certain features in common. Discover the parts of a typical adult bug below.

ANTENNAE are used for touching, smelling and telling temperature.

SIMPLE EYES are sensitive to light.

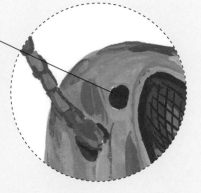

COMPOUND EYES are made up of many tiny lenses to help see objects and detect movement.

head

The *BODY* has three segments: a head, a middle part called a thorax and an abdomen.

thorax   abdomen

The *EXOSKELETON*, or outside skeleton, is a hard outer covering that protects the soft body.

forewing   hindwing

LEGS are used for walking. An insect has six jointed legs.

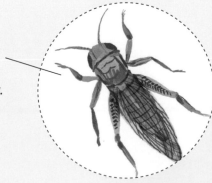

WINGS allow an insect to fly. Some insects have no wings. Others have one or two pairs.

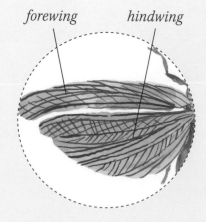

TRUE BUGS

Although this book is about insects, we sometimes call them "bugs." People often use the word *bug* to mean any tiny crawling or flying animal. In science, however, the term *true bug* means a specific kind of insect.

True bugs have a tubelike mouth for piercing plants and sucking up their juices. Some true bugs feed on animals. Often their forewings are partly solid and partly clear. They undergo incomplete metamorphosis. (Turn to page 11 to find out how!)

TREEHOPPER BUG

HARLEQUIN BUG

WATER STRIDER

BOXELDER BUG

MILKWEED BUG

STINK BUG

ASSASSIN BUG

CICADA

STRANGE BUGS

Mantids use camouflage to catch their dinner. Their bright green color and long, slender bodies make them very hard to see when they are hiding on a plant, ready to pounce. The long, folded front legs of a praying mantis are great for grabbing and holding on to insects.

MANTID

Insect Impostors

When you're bug-watching, you'll find lots of little creatures that look like insects but are not. Spiders, centipedes, snails, earthworms and pillbugs are some insect look-alikes. If you're not sure what you've found is a real insect, use these pages to help you spot the impostor!

ARACHNIDS

All arachnids have eight legs, two body segments and only simple eyes. They have no antennae or wings. Arachnids do not undergo metamorphosis.

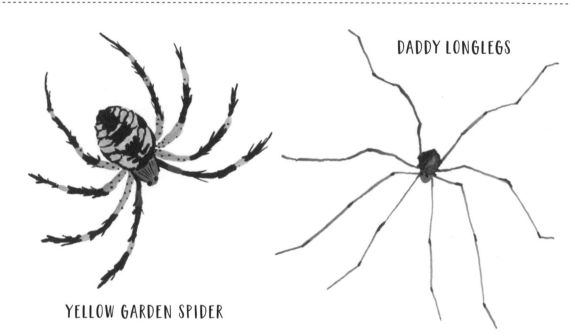

DADDY LONGLEGS

YELLOW GARDEN SPIDER

MYRIAPODS

The word *myriapod* means "many legs." Different species can have anywhere from 10 to 750 legs. Myriapods are segmented and have one pair of antennae. Most of them have simple eyes.

HOUSE CENTIPEDE

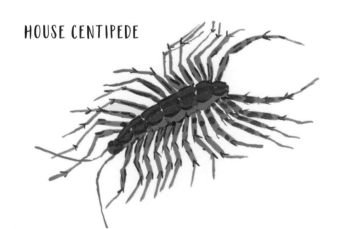

MILLIPEDE

GASTROPODS

Snails and slugs belong to a group called gastropods. These animals have a single shell (snails) or no shell (slugs), and one or two pairs of antennae with eyes on the ends. They move on a single muscular foot, often leaving a slimy trail.

GARDEN SNAIL

SLUG

ANNELIDS

COMMON EARTHWORM

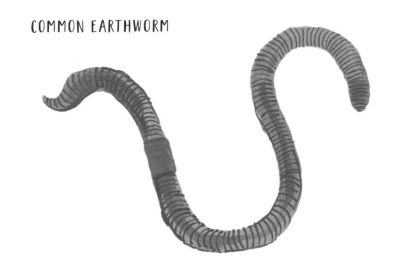

Annelids are a large group of soft-bodied, segmented worms. Instead of legs, they have pairs of bristlelike growths on each segment to help them move around.

MEDICINAL LEECH

ISOPODS

Sometimes called mini armadillos, isopods have hard segmented exoskeletons, two pairs of antennae and seven pairs of jointed legs. They breathe using the five pairs of jointed appendages (body parts that grow out of an insect's body) on the abdomen.

PILLBUG

WOOD LOUSE (SOWBUG)

A Bug's Life

When you were born, you were a small version of the person you are today. But most insects completely change their size, shape and color as they go through their life cycle. These changes are called metamorphosis. An adult insect may live for a few days or many years, depending on the species. Most adult insects live for a week or so, just long enough to mate and lay eggs. An average female insect lays 100 to 200 eggs in her short lifetime.

COMPLETE METAMORPHOSIS

Complete metamorphosis has four stages: egg, larva, pupa and adult. Insects such as flies, beetles, butterflies, bees and ants go through these four stages.

◗ *An adult insect lays her eggs.*

② *A larva hatches from an egg, then eats and grows.*

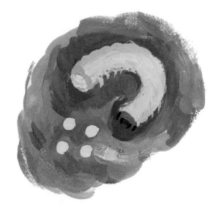

◗ *A pupa (called a chrysalis for butterflies) forms as a protective covering, or cocoon. Inside, the insect is usually inactive and doesn't eat while its adult body forms.*

④ *The pupa splits, and the adult climbs out.*

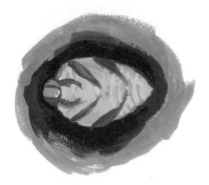

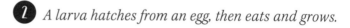

INCOMPLETE METAMORPHOSIS

Some insects, such as grasshoppers, earwigs and dragonflies, go through only three stages. This type of life cycle is called incomplete metamorphosis. The stages are egg, nymph and adult.

1 *An adult insect lays her eggs.*

2 *Nymphs hatch from the eggs. They do not have wings yet. Nymphs eat, grow and molt (shed their exoskeletons) until they are ready to change into adults.*

3 *During the last molt, a winged adult is produced. It will search for a mate after only a few hours.*

STRANGE BUGS

A few insects, such as silverfish, hatch from their eggs as tiny versions of the adults. They simply grow larger over time until they reach adult size. As they grow, their outer layer frequently becomes too tight, and they molt to reveal a new, larger skin underneath.

ADULT SILVERFISH

NYMPH SILVERFISH

A Bug's Home

The home you live in is probably made out of brick, concrete, steel, wood or stone. Insects have homes made from wood, paper, plants, soil, mud, shells and many other materials found in nature. Here are some insect homes to watch for in your neighborhood.

🐞 *When froghopper nymphs, called spittlebugs, hatch from their eggs, they begin sucking up plant juices. They turn some of the juices into a bubbly home where the bugs hide while they develop into adults.*

🐞 *If you could climb inside an anthill, you'd see many tunnels and rooms. The workers dig out the tunnels and carry the unwanted soil or sand up to the surface of the ground, making the little hill you see.*

🐞 *If you find a leaf with a see-through patch or path in it, then you've found the home of a leaf-mining insect. The larvae of many different kinds of insects eat their way around the insides of leaves, between the outer layers.*

🐞 *When the larva of a gall insect burrows into a plant, the plant grows around the insect. This growth is called a gall. Inside this plant home, the larva eats all winter long, safe from the cold and hidden from predators.*

🐞 *Honeybees build their hives in hollow spaces, such as tree trunks or fallen logs. They line the inside of the hive with a wax made from their bodies.*

🐞 *Eastern yellow jacket wasps nest in underground areas, such as under tree stumps.*

13

Bugs in the Water

If you go wading in a marsh, pond or river, you may see some of the incredible insects that live there. Some insects live on top of the water, while others live just below the surface or even at the bottom.

Aquatic insects have special ways of breathing underwater. And they have amazing ways of moving through water, too! Check out the special features of a few aquatic insects on this page.

RAT-TAILED MAGGOTS *have tubelike siphons that reach above the water, like a built-in snorkel.*

BACKSWIMMERS *swim on their backs, which are shaped like the bottom of a sailboat.*

DAMSELFLY NYMPHS *have gills that take oxygen directly from the water, like fish gills do.*

WATER STRIDERS *live on top of the pond.*

MOSQUITO LARVAE *hang upside down, just below the water's surface.*

WATER BOATMEN *have an extra-long pair of legs that they use like oars to row themselves around.*

DIVING BEETLES *trap an air bubble under their wing covers and use it like a scuba diver's tank when they swim underwater.*

DRAGONFLY NYMPHS *rest on the bottom of the pond. To breathe, they pump water in and out of their gills. By pumping faster, they can propel themselves forward.*

15

Bugs in Spring

Spring is a perfect time of year to start watching bugs in your neighborhood. Newly emerged flying insects often form mating swarms in the air. On the ground, ants, beetles and other bugs are waking up and coming out of hibernation.

GIANT SILKWORM MOTHS

From April to June, look for adult giant silkworm moths emerging from their cocoons in fields, woods and backyards. The name silkworm moth comes from the many layers of silk the caterpillars spin to make their cocoons. Silkworm moths don't have any mouthparts, so they never eat and live for only about a week. They spend their short lives looking for a mate, mating and laying eggs so that more moths will be born.

HONEYBEES

Check early spring flowers for honeybees. They are gathering food and pollinating the flowers at the same time. A group of honeybees needs to collect nectar from 60 000 to 90 000 individual flowers to make a thimbleful of honey. Some hardworking hives make up to 900 g (2 lb.) of honey per day. Honeybees are essential to the successful growth of many fruits and vegetables. Bees visit hundreds of flowers a day to feed on their pollen and nectar. The pollen from one flower sticks to a bee's hairy body and some gets rubbed off on the next flower the bee visits. This is how the flower gets pollinated. A flower must be pollinated before fruit can grow.

Bugs in Summer

When temperatures rise in the summer, bug activity really heats up! You'll start to see more ants, flies, moths and mosquitoes.

You don't need to see in the dark to find insects on a summer's night. At bedtime, open your curtains and turn on the light. Soon you'll see insects flying to your window, and you may hear them landing on the screen. Look for moths, june beetles, mosquitoes and other night fliers. You can also see nocturnal insects (ones that are active at night) gathered around porch lights and streetlights after dark.

LIGHT UP THE NIGHT

On a summer's night, set up a light outdoors to attract nocturnal insects. Then, use a magnifying glass to get a close-up look at these interesting creatures. Look for hard-winged beetles; soft, scaly-winged moths; and clear-winged mosquitoes and crane flies. How do these bugs compare to each other? Use this page, along with a field guide, to identify some of the insects you see.

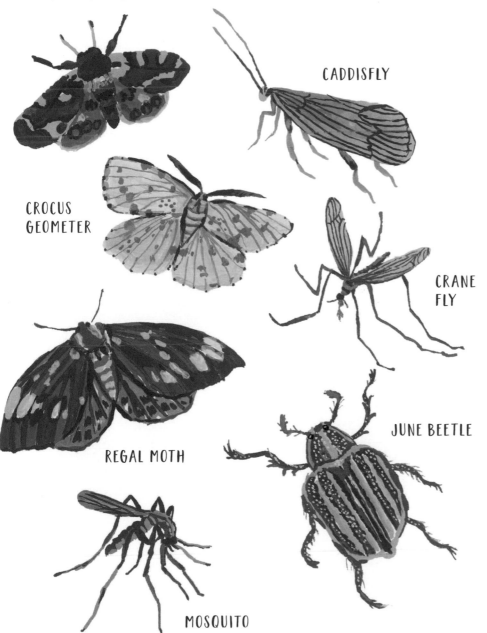

GARDEN TIGER MOTH

CADDISFLY

CROCUS GEOMETER

CRANE FLY

REGAL MOTH

JUNE BEETLE

MOSQUITO

FIREFLY (MALE)

FIREFLY (FEMALE)

Bugs in Fall

As the cold weather approaches, you might start to notice fewer and less-active bugs. You may know that many birds migrate, or fly south, when winter approaches. But did you know that some insects migrate, too? Insects migrate for several reasons: to avoid a cold or dry season, or to find food or a mate. In the fall, certain kinds of dragonflies, moths and beetles migrate long distances.

MONARCH MIGRATION

Most butterflies form chrysalides to survive winter, but some butterflies fly south to warmer weather. Every year in late summer and fall, masses of monarchs leave their breeding grounds in New England, Ontario and around the Great Lakes and head south to their winter home in the Sierra Madre mountains of central Mexico. There, millions of monarchs rest in evergreen trees, sometimes called butterfly trees.

In late February, the monarchs start to return northward. During the flight, the butterflies mate and most of the males die. Many of the females lay their eggs on the way back and also die. The young hatch from these eggs, develop into butterflies and continue the northward trip. Some females make it all the way back north to lay their eggs on milkweed plants.

Monarchs that breed in the valleys of the Rocky Mountains in Idaho and Montana migrate to California, between San Francisco and San Diego, during the winter months.

STRANGE BUGS

Some insects, such as butterflies and flies, have their taste buds on their legs and feet. While walking, they can find very small bits of food and taste them before eating. Tasting with their feet helps some butterflies choose the right place to lay their eggs. Eggs must be laid on a plant that the caterpillars can feed on as soon as they hatch.

RED-SPOTTED
PURPLE BUTTERFLY

21

Bugs in Winter

Once you know where to go and what to look for, you'll discover that bug-watching is a great year-round hobby. If you live in the southern United States, you can find bugs any time of year. But if you live where the winters are cold and snowy, bug-watching in winter becomes a real adventure.

Insects are cold-blooded, which means they depend on the temperature outside their bodies to warm them up and keep them active and alert. Mild days are the best times to bug-watch in winter.

Adult mourningcloak butterflies hibernate during the cold weather but leave their shelter of bark or rotting logs on sunny winter days.

When temperatures rise above freezing, carpenter ants that hibernate inside dead trees begin carving out new chambers in the wood.

Check around trees for tiny black specks on the snow — they are probably snow fleas.

HIBERNATING INSECTS

When you are searching for active insects, you may find some inactive ones, too. Most insects in the north hibernate to survive the cold. They stop growing and usually don't eat or move around until warmer weather arrives. How many of these hibernating insects can you find? Remember not to disturb them.

Some moth caterpillars spin cocoons in rolled-up leaves.

Check twigs and plant stems for insect galls, eggs or butterfly chrysalides.

Rotting logs are like apartment buildings for insects. Roll a log over or carefully peek under the bark to see if anything is hibernating there. Put the log back the way you found it.

In late winter, when the snow starts to melt, peek under the leaves that cover the soil. Look for slow-moving ladybugs and other beetles that have spent the winter sheltering there.

23

Beginner Bug-Watching

One of the best ways to find insects is to go for a hike on your hands and knees. Look carefully, since most insects are tiny and many are well camouflaged — they are colored or shaped to blend in with their surroundings. Remember to let the insects go back to their homes once you've looked at them.

HABITAT

- Does it live aboveground, underground or underwater? Or on a plant or tree?
- Does it build a home?

wasp nest *termite tower*

anthill *tent caterpillar web*

BEHAVIOR

- How does it move? Does it fly, hop, jump or crawl?
- Does it make a noise? If so, what does it sound like?
- Is it active during the day or at night?

BODY

- Are the antennae long or short? Are they segmented or smooth?

long *short* *segmented* *smooth*

- Does it have a mouthpart? If so, what does it look like?

chewing *sucking* *lapping*

- Does it have wings? How many?
- Is the body hairy or smooth? Does it have any special markings?
- Does it have a narrow or wide waist?

narrow *wide*

- How many legs does it have? Are they short or long?

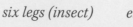

six legs (insect) *eight legs (arachnid)* *many legs (myriapod)*

- Are there one or more taillike appendages?

BUTTERFLY OR MOTH?

wings rest upright

straight, thin antennae

wings rest downward

bushy, feather-like antennae

small, narrow body

active during the day

BUTTERFLY

large, hairy body

active at night

MOTH

DRAGONFLY OR DAMSELFLY?

wings rest straight out

wings rest folded over their backs

short, thick body

long, slender body

DRAGONFLY

DAMSELFLY

BEE OR WASP?

large, hairy body

thick, hairy legs

long, smooth body

slender legs

BEES AND WASPS CAN STING, SO DON'T GET TOO CLOSE TO THEIR HOMES.

broad wings

wide waist

narrow wings

narrow waist

BEE

WASP

A BUG-WATCHER'S BACKPACK

GARDEN TROWEL

NET

MAGNIFYING GLASS

CAMERA

FIELD GUIDE

NOTES

NOTEBOOK

PENCIL

25

More Strange Bugs

PERFECT DISGUISE

Shaped and colored just like twigs, walking sticks blend in perfectly with the shrubs or trees where they live and feed. Most are wingless, and they range in size from 1¼ cm (½ in.) to 15 cm (6 in.) or more.

WALKING STICK

STINK BUG

A REAL STINKER

When a stink bug is in danger from a predator, such as a bird or lizard, it releases a bad odor from holes in its abdomen. The stinky shot can repel the enemy and save the bug's life.

HAIL THE QUEEN

A termite colony is centered on the queen, which lays all of the eggs for the colony. Termite queens have the longest life span of any insect, some living up to 50 years. At maturity, a queen can produce up to 40 000 eggs per day.

TERMITE QUEEN

FAKE EYES

Some insects, such as the tiger swallowtail caterpillar, have fake eyes to fool predators into attacking a less vulnerable part of the insect's body. Their real eyes are very small and hard for predators to find.

TIGER SWALLOWTAIL

THREE "TAILS"

Silverfish are a common household insect without wings. These quick moving, silvery bugs slither around cool, damp places like bathrooms or under sinks. They have three taillike appendages at the end of their abdomen, which they may use for feeling.

SILVERFISH

R.I.P.

Burying beetles are the undertakers of the insect world. When they find a small dead animal, such as a mouse, they burrow beneath it. The dead body eventually sinks down below ground level and is covered over with earth. The female lays her eggs nearby and the larvae and adults feed on the buried corpse.

BURYING BEETLE

Endangered Bugs

Insects need food, shelter and a place to reproduce, like all wildlife. When people drain wetlands, log forests and plow prairie habitats, millions of insects lose their homes and die. Insects are also destroyed when we use poisons called pesticides on farms, along roadsides and in parks and backyard gardens. And collectors may threaten the populations of rare and beautiful butterflies and moths.

When we kill insects, there is less food for insect-eating birds, reptiles, mammals and amphibians.

Here are some things you can do to help protect insects:

🐞 Always safely return insects to the wild after you've had a good look at them.

🐞 Learn to get along with insects. Everyone swats at annoying mosquitoes, but most insects are harmless, so don't hurt them.

🐞 Put up an insect feeder (like the one on the facing page!) or plant flowers in a pot or garden to give some local bees and butterflies a treat.

🐞 Encourage your grown-ups to ask a gardening store about natural ways to control insects near your home instead of using harmful pesticides.

🐞 Research what insects in your province or state are listed as endangered, threatened or rare. Write to the government to ask what is being done to protect them.

🐞 Raise money for conservation groups that protect threatened insects and their habitats. Here are a few ideas:

- have a yard sale

- collect donations for your class to clean up a local park

- sell tickets for a guided walk led by a naturalist (a nature expert) through a local park

NORTHERN BARRENS
TIGER BEETLE

PRAIRIE MOLE CRICKET

KARNER BLUE BUTTERFLY

MAKE AN INSECT FEEDER

Make your very own insect feeder (like a bird feeder) to hang outside your home. Then watch how butterflies, moths, bees, flies and other nectar-loving insects drink at your feeder.

1 Cut a strip of sponge 4 cm (1½ in.) wide and 15 cm (6 in.) long.

2 Ask an adult to cut a 2 cm (¾ in.) hole near the bottom of the bottle.

3 Cut a piece of twine 20 cm (8 in.) long. Tie one end around the stone and the other end around the sponge.

4 Push the stone and twine through the hole in the bottle. Then push the sponge almost all the way through, leaving 2 cm (¾ in.) sticking out of the hole.

6 Tie a long piece of twine or wire tightly around the bottle, and hang it outside near a window, where you can watch it. If you have a garden, tie your feeder to a post or tree trunk to attract pollinators to your flowers, fruits and vegetables.

5 Use the funnel to pour the sugar into the bottle. Over a sink, fill the bottle three-quarters full with water. Then put the lid on and quickly turn the bottle upside down. The water level should be just below the hole. Carefully shake the bottle to dissolve the sugar.

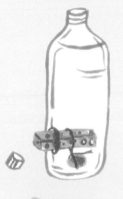

The twine will keep the water moving up to the sponge.

Glossary

abdomen: the end body part of an adult insect. It contains the reproductive organs.

annelid: a segmented worm, such as an earthworm or leech

antennae: a pair of movable sensory organs for feeling surroundings that are attached to an insect's head. Some insects also use them for tasting, smelling, hearing, detecting humidity and gauging wind speed.

appendage: a body part that grows out of an insect's body, such as a leg or antenna

aquatic: living in water

arachnid: an eight-legged, wingless invertebrate, such as a spider or scorpion

camouflage: blending into the background, usually due to color or shape

chrysalis: the hard, solid-shelled covering of a butterfly in the pupa stage

cocoon: the soft, silky covering of many insects in the pupa stage, including moths

cold-blooded: not able to maintain a constant body temperature internally. Cold-blooded insects rely on the outside temperature to heat and cool their bodies.

complete metamorphosis: an insect's change in size, shape and color in four stages: egg, larva, pupa and adult

compound eye: an eye made up of many individual lenses capable of forming an image

exoskeleton: the hard outer covering that protects an insect's soft body

forewings: the front pair of wings, if the insect has two pairs

gall: an abnormal growth on a plant, often caused by gall insect damage

gastropod: a single-shelled, or shell-less, mollusk with a single muscular foot. Includes snails and slugs.

habitat: the natural environment where an organism lives. It provides shelter, food, water and protection.

hibernate: to find shelter and become inactive, often during cold or dry weather

hindwings: the rear pair of wings, if the insect has two pairs

incomplete metamorphosis: an insect's change in size, shape and color in three stages: egg, nymph and adult

isopod: a small invertebrate with a hard, segmented exoskeleton, seven pairs of legs, two pairs of antennae and five pairs of abdominal appendages. Includes wood lice and pillbugs.

larva: the pre-adult form of an insect between the egg and pupa stages

life cycle: an insect's stages from egg to adult

metamorphosis: an insect's change in size, shape and color as it goes through its life cycle from egg to adult. Metamorphosis happens in three or more very different stages.

migrate: to travel a long distance, usually to find food or avoid cold or dry weather

molt: to shed the exoskeleton

myriapod: a segmented invertebrate with many legs, one pair of antennae and simple eyes. Includes centipedes and millipedes.

nocturnal: active during the night

nymph: the pre-adult, wingless form of an insect during incomplete metamorphosis.

pesticide: a chemical used to kill or control an unwanted plant or animal

pollination: the transfer of pollen from one flower to another

predator: an animal that feeds on, or preys upon, another animal

pupa: the third stage of complete metamorphosis

simple eye: a light-sensitive eye with one lens

siphon: the tubelike mouthpart of moths and butterflies used to suck nectar from tubular flowers. It can roll up under the insect's head when not in use.

thorax: the middle body part of an adult insect. The legs and wings are attached here.

true bugs: the group of insects that have specialized sucking mouthparts and undergo incomplete metamorphosis

Index